tibits at home

© 2012
AT Verlag, Aarau and Munich

Concept: Annette Gröbly, Anna Staiger Eichenberger
Recipes: tibits AG, adapted and prepared by Stefan Staiger
Copy: Bettina Weber, Zurich
Translation: Frauke Watson and Kaye Holland
Photography: Sylvan Müller, Lucerne, www.sylvanmueller.ch
Styling: Karin Böhnke, Lucerne, www.hochrot.ch
Foodstyling: Oliver Roth, Zurich, www.food-styling.ch
Wallpaper: Designers Guild London, represented by Wohn-In Küsnacht
Flowers: Martin Grossenbacher, Zurich

Graphic design: Stefan Haas, Lucerne, www.haasgrafik.ch
Picture editing: Brigitte Hürzeler, Lucerne
Printing and binding: FINIDR, Czech Republic

ISBN 978-3-03800-734-0

www.at-verlag.ch
www.tibits.ch
www.tibits.co.uk

stylish
vegetarian
cuisine

tibits
at
home

tibits

We dedicate this book to our families and the tibits staff,
who have been with us every step of the way for the last 10 years,
offering company and support on our culinary journey.

A warm "thank you" to our faithful patrons for all their heartfelt
compliments and their valuable tips and advice – always welcome.

We would also like to thank the four families who kindly gave us
access to their homes, to shoot the photographs for this book,
and everyone who contributed to the project.

All recipes serve 4,
unless otherwise specified.

welcome

Over the years, many of our patrons have been asking for the recipes of their favourite dishes. For a long time, we have guarded them jealously. However to celebrate our 10-year anniversary, we have decided to lift the lids of our pans and allow you a peek inside. We are proud to present 50 of our favourite recipes. They are easy to make and ideal – be it for a quick tasty snack or a big dinner with friends – which is why we called this book 'tibits at home'. The recipes are easy to follow and are as much fun to make, as they are to eat. Four of our most loyal customers have kindly agreed to open their doors, for our photographers. They are very different personalities, but all are equally inspired hosts – and we hope that their enjoyment of good food and company and their gift for entertainment, will get your culinary and creative juices flowing.

We hope you will enjoy recreating our recipes at home!
All the best
The Frei brothers and the Hiltl family

the world goes greener

Finally – just when you think that you can't abide another cold and wintry day full of snowflakes, there it is. A little reluctantly and pale perhaps, but – here comes the sun! Luxuriously, we squint into the first warm rays that tickle our nose. We meet the sun with a big smile as she coaxes us back to life. Suddenly, we feel the urge to throw the balcony doors wide open, to take a deep breath and to walk outside in the fresh air in order to watch nature as she awakens from her slumber. We want to see buds opening everywhere and the world go greener and more colourful and joyful every day. The temperament and the colours of springtime are contagious: they put us in a good mood. Spring cuisine, first and foremost, needs to be fresh, seasonal and healthy.

A sweet and spicy drink – healthy,
delicious and rather attractive!

ginger, carrot and apple juice

1 Peel the ginger and lemons. Wash and peel
the carrots. Cut the apples and the fennel into halves
or quarters so that they fit into the juice extractor.
2 Put all the ingredients into the juice extractor.
Stir the juice well, leave to settle for 5 minutes and
then skim off the foam.

3 Put the juice in the refrigerator. Before
serving, stir well.

Tip: sweeten to taste, with maple syrup.

Makes 1 litre

Preparation time

15 minutes

100 g fresh ginger

8 lemons

1.2 kg carrots

2 apples (Jonagold; 200 g)

2 fennel bulbs (200 g)

A taste of spring
to be served hot or cold

pea soup with fresh mint

1 Peel and finely chop the shallots. Wash the mint, pick off the leaves and cut into fine strips.
2 If you use fresh peas, peel then blanch in boiling salted water, drain and rinse under running cold water. If using frozen peas, this step is unnecessary.
3 Wash and peel the potatoes and cut into 1.5 cm dice.
4 Sweat the shallots in the hot olive oil and sprinkle over the mint. Then add peas and potato and cook until they draw water. Pour in the vegetable stock and simmer for 10 minutes.

5 Puree all the ingredients in the food processor or use a hand blender, then pass through a fine sieve.
6 Add the cream and bring to the boil, very briefly. Season to taste with sea salt and white pepper.

Tip: serve with peeled and finely chopped tomatoes and garnish with a fresh mint leaf or two.

Preparation time	2 shallots	3 tbsp extra virgin olive oil
30 minutes	2 sprigs of fresh mint	700 ml vegetable stock
	1 kg fresh (unshelled) peas or	50 ml whipping cream
	400 g frozen peas	sea salt and freshly
	200 g potatoes	ground white pepper

olive and tomato sandwich

1 Puree the tofu, rice mayonnaise and olives in the
food processor or with the hand blender to a fine paste.
2 Wash and peel the carrot, cut into 0.5 cm slices,
then into 0.5 cm dice.
3 Wash the basil and cut into fine strips.
4 Combine the olive paste with the tomato pesto,
basil and diced carrots. Mix well.
5 Cut the bread rolls in half, lengthwise. Spread the
lower half with the paste.
6 Slice the tomatoes and arrange on top of the paste.
Sprinkle with rocket leaves and put the upper half
of the bread roll on top. Cut the sandwich into
halves, diagonally.

Preparation time	Olive paste (makes 800 g)		1	carrot (120 g)	Sandwich	
15 minutes	200 g	tofu	1 bunch	of basil	4	bread rolls (ciabatta and wholegrain)
	100 g	rice mayonnaise	150 g	tomato pesto	200 g	olive paste
		(available from health food shops)		(see p136)	2	tomatoes
	170 g	black olives, pitted			40 g	rocket

bulgur and flat bean salad

1 Bring the bulgur, water and sea salt to the boil, stirring constantly. Cook for 8 minutes until all the water has been absorbed. Put into a bowl and refrigerate for 1 hour.
2 Wash the cherry tomatoes and cut into halves. Wash the flat beans and cut into 4 cm lengths.
3 Cook the beans in salted water until tender (approximately 20 minutes). Drain immediately and rinse under cold running water.
4 Grate the ginger and mix all the sauce ingredients together. Season with salt and pepper.
5 Break up the bulgur with a fork and mix with the flat beans and the cherry tomatoes. Add the sauce and stir well.

Tip: bulgur is a parboiled and dried durum wheat that has been cleaned and ground. It has a mild nutty taste and is very filling and nutritious, with comparatively few calories. You can buy fine, medium and course ground bulgur.

Preparation time	120 g	bulgur		Sauce
30 minutes	240 ml	water		15 g freshly ground ginger
	1 tsp	sea salt (to cook the bulgur)		7 tbsp extra virgin olive oil
	150 g	cherry tomatoes		7 tbsp white balsamic vinegar
	150 g	green flat beans		1 tbsp tomato paste
	1 tsp	sea salt (to cook the beans)		½ tsp hot curry powder
				½ tsp mild paprika
				½ tsp ground coriander
				freshly ground salt and pepper

Wonderfully refreshing and a feast for the eyes!

peppered tofu
with cucumbers

1 Wash and peel the cucumbers. Trim off the ends
and cut into 0.5 cm slices.
2 Cut the tofu in 0.5 cm slices and sprinkle with
pepper on both sides.
3 Arrange on a serving platter or on individual plates,
alternating the cucumber and tofu slices.
4 Mix the sauce ingredients well and drizzle over
the salad.
5 Sprinkle with fresh dill greens, right before serving.

Tip: arrange on fresh baguette slices and serve
with the aperitif.

Preparation time			Salad dressing	
20 minutes	2	cucumbers (500 g)	7 tbsp	rapeseed oil
	500 g	tofu nature or tofu provençal	3 tbsp	white balsamic vinegar
		freshly ground pepper	1 tsp	sea salt
			1 bunch	of dill

The ancient cereal from South America
is becoming increasingly popular in Europe

quinoa with curry and cranberries

1 Rinse the quinoa under running water.
2 Bring the salted water to a boil, stir in the quinoa
and simmer for about 20 minutes. Pour into a sieve
and leave to drain well.
3 Mix all the other ingredients, except for the
cranberries, in a bowl. Add the quinoa and mix well.
4 Add the cranberries, mix well and keep in the
refrigerator until ready to serve.

Tip: you can prepare the quinoa the evening
before and leave to drain in the refrigerator.
Quinoa is gluten-free and rich in protein.

Preparation time	100 g	white quinoa	1 tbsp	curry powder, hot or mild
30 minutes	4 tbsp	white balsamic vinegar	½ tsp	ground coriander
	3 tbsp	rapeseed oil	1 tbsp	fine raw cane sugar
	25 g	freshly ground ginger	50 ml	coconut milk
	1 tsp	fine sea salt	50 g	dried cranberries
	1 tsp	turmeric		

coconut and peanut fritters

1 Mash the tofu into a fine paste, using your hands.
2 Chop the peanuts with a knife or coarsely grind using a hand blender. Work the peanuts, turmeric and curry powder into the tofu until the paste has taken on the colour of the turmeric. Add the coconut flakes, mix well and season with salt and pepper.
3 Using an ice cream scoop, shape the paste into balls and evenly fry in hot oil (170°C) until golden brown. Alternatively, evenly coat with oil and bake in a hot oven at 160°C.

Tip: instead of the curry powder, use freshly ground ginger.

Makes 20-25 balls
Preparation time
30 minutes

500 g	soft tofu
200 g	unsalted, roasted peanuts
1 tbsp	turmeric
1 tbsp	hot curry powder
100 g	coconut flakes
	fine sea salt and pepper, freshly ground
	peanut oil for frying

25

All is ready –
the guests are welcome

inspiration

One of our favourite recipes
and a wonderful source of protein

soybeans with lemon dressing

1 Bring water and sea salt to the boil, add soybeans and cook until tender (10-12 minutes). Drain and rinse thoroughly, under cold running water.
2 Chop the sundried tomatoes. Wash the red pepper, remove the seeds and chop into 2 cm dice. Wash and drain the rocket. Put everything into a bowl, add the soybeans and mix well.
3 Wash the lemons, grate the zest and press out the juice.
4 Mix the lemon juice and zest with the other dressing ingredients and drizzle over the salad. Mix well and refrigerate.
5 Roast the pine nuts in a dry pan and sprinkle over the salad, just before serving.

The soybean is a species of legume. It is an important source of protein and vegetable oil and, as such, one of the most important crop plants worldwide. There are many varieties of soybeans – white, green, black and red – and they are available dried or frozen. All are rich in unsaturated fats and low in cholesterol and can therefore help to reduce heart diseases.

Preparation time	2 l	water		Dressing
25 minutes	1 tsp	sea salt	2	lemons
	600 g	frozen green soybeans	4 tbsp	rapeseed oil
	100 g	sundried tomatoes (in oil)	2 tbsp	lemon oil
	1	red pepper	1 tsp	sea salt
	100 g	rocket	1 tbsp	roasted pine nuts

white asparagus with orange sauce

1 Peel the asparagus, trim off the ends and cut into 4–5 cm lengths.

2 Bring the water, sea salt, rapeseed oil, lemon juice and sugar to the boil, add the asparagus and cook for 15 minutes until tender but firm. Drain well.

3 Meanwhile bring the milk, cream, orange juice and chilli oil to the boil, add turmeric and sea salt and simmer for 2 minutes. Mix the cornflour with the cold water and add to the sauce. Simmer for about 1 minute until it thickens, then mix with a hand blender.

4 Add the asparagus to the sauce and cook for 5 minutes.

5 Sprinkle with finely chopped chives and serve immediately.

Preparation time	1.5 kg white asparagus	Sauce	2 tbsp cornflour
40 minutes	2-4 l water	150 ml milk	2 tbsp cold water
	4 tbsp rapeseed oil	200 ml whipping cream	30 g finely chopped chives
	1 tbsp lemon juice	150 ml freshly pressed orange juice	
	1 tbsp white sugar	(2-3 oranges)	
		1 tsp chilli oil	
		½ tsp turmeric	
		1 tsp fine sea salt	

red thai vegetables

1 Wash the beans and cut into 4 cm pieces. Cook in saltwater until tender. Then drain and rinse immediately under cold running water.

2 Wash the courgettes and cut into 2 cm dice. Wash the red pepper, remove the seeds and cut into 2 cm dice. Clean the mushrooms, remove any traces of soil and the ends.

3 Heat the peanut oil and sweat the red pepper, mushrooms and courgettes for 3-4 minutes. Drain in a sieve.

4 Meanwhile mix the coconut milk with the vegetable stock and the curry paste, and bring to the boil.

5 Add the vegetables and cook for another 5 minutes. Add salt and pepper, to taste. Serve with basmati rice with herbs (recipe on p136) and the finely chopped Thai basil.

Tip: you can also add freshly ground ginger.

Preparation time	300 g	cocoa beans	6 tbsp	peanut oil
30 minutes	200 g	courgettes	400 ml	coconut milk
	200 g	red pepper	100 ml	vegetable stock
	300 g	small mushrooms (button mushrooms	80 g	red curry paste
		are best, followed by oyster mushrooms		sea salt and black pepper, freshly ground
		or shiitake mushrooms)	1 bunch	of Thai basil

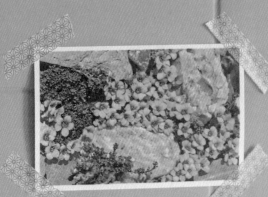

coconut and pineapple tiramisu

1 Cover the bottom of a 17 × 22 cm gratin dish with ladyfingers and pour over the coconut milk.
2 Cut the pineapple into 1.5 cm dice and mix well with the sugar. Spread evenly over the ladyfingers.
3 Scrape out the vanilla pulp. Mix the mascarpone, cream, sugar and vanilla pulp in a cold stainless steel bowl, until it is smooth and fluffy. Spread evenly over the pineapple and smooth out.

4 Refrigerate for at least 4 hours and serve dusted with cocoa powder.

Tip: prepare the tiramisu a day in advance to allow the ladyfingers to become soft and moist.

Preparation time
20 minutes

100 g	ladyfingers
100 ml	coconut milk
160 g	pineapple
3 tbsp	fine raw cane sugar
250 g	mascarpone
50 ml	whipping cream
5 tbsp	fine raw cane sugar
1	bourbon vanilla pod
1 tbsp	cocoa powder, sweetened

We get a lot of compliments for this delicious cake!

london cheesecake

1 Chop the whole-grain biscuits and walnuts finely. Add sugar and oil and mix well. Spread the mixture evenly into a 15 × 20 cm gratin dish.

2 Mix all the other ingredients in a cold stainless steel bowl to a smooth and compact cream, then spread over the biscuit mix.

3 Bake the cake in the preheated oven at 180°C for 25-30 minutes until golden brown.

Tip: serve with whipped cream and fresh seasonal berries. Blanc battu is a thick, viscous curd cheese. As it is made from skimmed milk, it has a very low fat content.

Preparation time	100 g	whole-grain biscuits	50 g	probiotic yoghurt
15 minutes	30 g	walnuts	80 g	crème fraiche
Baking time	1 tbsp	fine raw cane sugar	250 g	blanc battu
30 minutes	5 tbsp	rapeseed oil	100 g	fine raw cane sugar
			1	bourbon vanilla pod, pulp
			2	eggs
			1 tbsp	cornflour
			70 ml	whole milk

sum

mer

summertime

When the sky is blue and the temperature is balmy, somehow everything becomes a little easier and there is a positively Mediterranean joie de vivre in the air. The warm weather invites us to linger outside until midnight, counting the stars in the sky. Life happens outside now: we enjoy long walks and bicycle rides, while barbecues are fired up all over the country. Speaking of which, forget serving the inevitable sausages and steaks and offer your guests something a little different instead. How about a delicious chilled soup, seasoned with the abundance of fresh herbs you have been growing since spring? Some refreshing ice tea with lemon balm, home grown, of course? In the summer, the body craves fresh and healthy food: think juicy fruit like melons, strawberries and peaches. Being out in the fresh air all day is hungry work, but during the summer season, our food should be light and easily digestible.

With a splash of grapefruit – a refreshing
summer drink for big and small dragons

dragon iced tea

1 Bring 400 ml water to the boil. Put the tea leaves into a filter bag or a tea infuser and pour the boiling water over the tea. Steep for 15 minutes and remove the tea leaves.
2 Squeeze the grapefruit (you need 300 ml pink juice and 400 ml white juice).
3 Mix the tea, grapefruit juice and elderflower syrup with the cold water and refrigerate until ready to serve.

Makes 10 glasses	Dragon tea mixture	400 ml water
2.5 l of ice tea	(freshly mixed in good tea shops)	2-3 pink grapefruit
Preparation time	25 g Oolong tea (green tea)	3-4 yellow grapefruit
15 minutes	6 g mint leaves	200 ml elderflower syrup
	2 g hibiscus leaves	1.2 l cold water

feta and cucumber sandwich

1 Cut the baguettes in half lengthwise and spread tomato pesto, on both halves. Cut the feta cheese, cucumber and tomatoes into thin slices. Drizzle the cucumber slices with balsamic vinegar.

2 Put the cheese, tomato and cucumber slices on the lower half of the bread rolls, in layers. Top with a few washed and drained rocket leaves. Cover with the top half of the baguette and cut into pieces, diagonally if desired.

Tip: add some pitted black olives, to taste.

Preparation time	2	baguettes
15 minutes	120 g	tomato pesto (recipe on p136)
	240 g	feta cheese
	120 g	tomatoes
	120 g	cucumber
	2 tbsp	white balsamic vinegar
	40 g	rocket leaves

tomato soup with lemongrass and coconut milk

1 Peel and finely chop the onions and garlic. Squash the lemongrass on a chopping board and chop finely.
2 Wash the leek, cut in half lengthwise and then chop into fine strips. Wash the tomatoes, remove the stem ends and chop into 3 cm dice.
3 Sweat the garlic, onions and lemongrass in the hot olive oil until transparent. Add the diced tomatoes, vegetable stock, ginger, lemon pepper, chilli oil and sea salt and simmer at low temperature for 20 minutes. Puree the soup in the food processor and pass through a sieve.
4 Add the coconut milk and the leek and lightly cook for another 5 minutes. Add sea salt and pepper, to taste.

Preparation time	1 small onion	½ tsp ginger powder
40 minutes	2 garlic cloves	½ tsp lemon pepper
	1 stalk lemongrass	1 tsp chilli oil
	200 g green leeks	1 tsp sea salt
	600 g fully ripened tomatoes	150 ml coconut milk
	3 tbsp extra virgin olive oil	freshly ground sea salt
	350 ml vegetable stock	and white pepper

Three classic Italian antipasti dishes, seasoned with fresh herbs

mixed vegetable antipasto

mushroom antipasto

1 Wash the peppers and the courgettes and chop into 2 cm dice. Remove the stem ends of the okra pods and cut them in half lengthwise. Chop the garlic finely.
2 Fry the garlic and okra in the hot olive oil, then add the rest of the vegetables and fry for another 6-8 minutes. Leave to cool slightly.
3 Mix the sauce ingredients and add to the slightly cooled vegetables. Let them infuse for about 1 hour.
4 Serve with finely chopped fresh basil.

Tip: you can also deep fry the okra pods for 3 minutes, at 170°C.

2	red and 2 yellow peppers (400 g)
5	courgettes (500 g)
100 g	okra
1	garlic clove
5 tbsp	extra virgin olive oil
	Sauce
80 g	tomato pesto (recipe on p136)
4 tbsp	water
4 tsp	sea salt
1 tsp	chilli oil
1 tbsp	balsamic vinegar
	fresh basil leaves

1 Clean the mushrooms (see tip), wash the peppers, remove the seeds and chop.
2 Cut the sundried tomatoes and the rocket into fine strips.
3 Chop the garlic and onions.
4 Heat up a frying pan, then add the olive oil. Sweat the garlic and onion until transparent. Add mushrooms and peppers and fry for another 3-4 minutes. Remove the pan from the heat, then add chilli oil and chilli flakes and leave to cool.
5 Season with balsamic vinegar and sea salt. Finally, add the sundried tomatoes and rocket leaves.

Tip: cut a thin slice off the mushroom stalk, then remove traces of dirt with kitchen paper or a special mushroom cleaning brush.

400 g	small white mushrooms
1	red and 1 yellow pepper
60 g	sundried tomatoes in oil
50 g	rocket leaves
1	small onion
1	garlic clove
100 ml	extra virgin olive oil
1 tsp	chilli oil
1-2 tsp	chilli flakes
5 tbsp	white balsamic vinegar
1 tsp	fine sea salt

aubergine antipasto

1 Wash the aubergines and chop into 2 cm dice.
2 Heat the olive oil and fry the aubergines for
6-8 minutes. Remove from pan and drizzle with salt.
3 Drain the sundried tomatoes and chop finely.
Add to the aubergines.
4 Mix oil, salt and pepper. Mix well with the
aubergines, cover and refrigerate.
5 Wash the rocket leaves and chop finely.
Mix with the aubergines right before serving.

Tip: you can use tomato pesto (recipe on p136)
instead of sundried tomatoes.

600 g	aubergines
120 ml	extra virgin olive oil
1 tsp	fine sea salt
50 g	sundried tomatoes in oil
50 g	rocket leaves
	Sauce
1 tsp	chilli oil
1 tbsp	white balsamic vinegar
	freshly ground salt and pepper

Preparation time
20 minutes, per recipe

If you love fresh parsley and mint, this is for you

tabouli middle-eastern style

1 Cook the bulgur in salted water for about 8 minutes, until all the water has been absorbed. Put into a bowl and refrigerate for 1 hour.
2 Pluck the mint and parsley leaves from the stems, wash and chop finely.
3 Wash the tomatoes, remove the stem ends and chop into 1 cm dice.

4 Mix the sauce ingredients and season with pepper.
5 Break up the bulgur with a fork. Add the tomatoes, spinach and herbs and mix carefully. Add the sauce and mix again.

Tabouli is a wonderfully refreshing and nutritious summer dish. We have used bulgur (parboiled and dried durum wheat) instead of the traditional couscous.

Preparation time			Sauce
25 minutes	120 g bulgur	150 g baby spinach leaves	1.5 lemons (juice)
	250 ml water	50 g fresh mint	100 ml extra virgin olive oil
	2 tsp fine sea salt	40 g fresh coriander (cilantro)	1 tbsp fine sea salt
		30 g broad leaf parsley	1-2 tbsp chilli oil
		400 g tomatoes	freshly ground white pepper

A hot and sweet summertime temptation

tofu and honey melon salad

1 Peel the melon and remove the seeds with a spoon. Cut the meat into 2.5 cm dice.
2 Wash and peel the carrots, cut into fine strips, then slice lengthwise and cut the slices into fine strips.
3 Chop the tofu into 1.5 cm dice and quickly fry until golden brown. Leave to cool.

4 Mix the tofu, melon and carrot.
5 Mix the dressing ingredients with the hand blender, in a stainless steel bowl. Drizzle the dressing over the salad, mix well, cover and refrigerate.
6 Drizzle with coconut flakes and serve immediately.

Preparation time	1 honey melon	Dressing	½ tsp curry powder
25 minutes	2 carrots	100 ml sweet chilli sauce	½ tsp mild chilli powder
	300 g tofu	2 tbsp red curry paste	½ tsp ground coriander
	8 tbsp rapeseed oil	1 tbsp freshly ground ginger	½ tsp cumin
		1 tsp fine sea salt	30 g toasted coconut flakes
		1 tbsp tomato paste	

Serves 6

Preparation time

15 minutes

Passion fruit syrup

22 passion fruit

1 lemon

160 g sugar

Per serving

5 tbsp passion fruit syrup

ice cubes

sparkling mineral water

1 slice of orange

passion fruit lemonade

1 Cut the passion fruit in halves and remove seeds and pulp, into a wide cooking pan.

2 Press the lemon. Add lemon juice and sugar to the pulp and bring to the boil, then simmer at a low temperature for 3 minutes. Remove from the stove and leave to cool for a few minutes, then pass through a sieve and refrigerate.

3 Pour the juice into tall glasses with ice cubes and top up with sparkling mineral water. Serve with a slice of orange.

Tip: fully ripened passion fruit are the most flavourful. The skin should be dark purple, leathery and wrinkly. This is an exclusive recipe developed by tibits and Hiltl together.

mini calzones

1 Mix the flour and the salt and make a hole in
the centre.
2 Mix the yeast with the sugar and 50 ml warm water and
pour the mixture into the hole. Stir in a little of the flour.
Cover and leave to rise for 15 minutes, in a warm place.
3 Add the rest of the water and the oil and quickly
knead into dough. Cover and leave to rise for another
30-40 minutes.
4 Preheat the oven to 180°C and cover a baking tray,
with baking paper.

5 Peel the garlic and onions and chop finely. Clean the
mushrooms and cut into thin slices. Cut the peppers in
halves, remove the seeds and chop into 0.5 cm dice. Cut
the chilli in halves, remove the seeds and chop finely.
6 Heat the olive oil in a frying pan and briefly sweat the
garlic and onion. Add mushrooms, peppers and chilli and
fry for 10 minutes until the liquid has been absorbed.
Remove from the stove and leave to cool.
7 Finely chop the oregano and basil and mix with the
vegetables. Season with sugar, salt and pepper.
8 Add tomato pesto and Parmesan cheese and mix
thoroughly.
9 Cut the dough into 16 portions. Roll them out
individually on a floured surface into 10 cm rounds
(2-3 mm thick).
10 Spoon the filling into the middle of the rounds,
leaving a 1 cm edge all around. Fold the rounds into
half-moon shapes, pressing the edges together carefully.
Trim into shape with the paste cutter.
11 Put the mini calzones on the baking tray, brush
sparingly with olive oil and sprinkle with a little paprika.
Bake in the preheated oven (at 180°C) for 15 minutes.

Tip: instead of Parmesan cheese, try finely chopped
mozzarella.

Makes approximately	Pizza dough	Filling	1 tsp sugar
16 mini calzones	500 g white flour	2 small onions	freshly ground fine sea salt
Preparation time	1 tsp salt	2 garlic cloves	and black pepper
for the dough	20 g fresh yeast	300 g mushrooms	2 tbsp tomato pesto (recipe on p136)
50 minutes	½ tsp sugar	150 g red peppers	100 g Parmesan cheese, grated
Preparation time	250 ml water, at room	2 green chilli	olive oil for brushing
for the calzones	temperature	2 tbsp extra virgin olive oil	paprika powder for sprinkling
30 minutes	4 tbsp olive oil	½ bunch oregano	
		½ bunch basil	

vegetable quiche, mediterranean style

1 Preheat the oven to 180°C. Spread the dough on a baking tray covered with baking paper and prick with a fork.

2 Spread the tomato pesto onto the dough and sprinkle with breadcrumbs and Parmesan cheese.

3 Wash the vegetables and chop into 1.5 cm dice. Fry the aubergines for 6 minutes in hot olive oil, then add the courgettes and fry for another 5 minutes.

Pour into a bowl and mix with the chopped tomatoes, season with sea salt and leave to cool for a while.

4 Mix the flan ingredients thoroughly.

5 Spread the vegetable mixture over the dough and pour the flan mixture on top.

6 Cook the quiche in the oven for 35-49 minutes. Leave to cool for 10 minutes and serve.

Tip: make the quiche with puff pastry, instead.

Serves 4	1	spelt pizza dough (see recipe on p137) or	300 g	aubergines	Flan mixture	
as a main course	1	wholegrain cake mixture, rolled out to a	300 g	courgettes	3	eggs
Serves 8		diameter of 33 cm	300 g	tomatoes	150 ml	whipping cream
as a starter	100 g	tomato pesto (see recipe on p136)	8 tbsp	extra virgin olive oil	75 g	blanc battu
Preparation time	2-3 tbsp	bread crumbs		sea salt	1 tbsp	fine sea salt
30 minutes	50 g	cheese (for example Gruyère), grated			1 tbsp	chilli oil
					1 tsp	freshly chopped oregano

indian samosas

1 Peel the potatoes and chop into 0.5 cm dice. Cook in salt water until tender, and drain.

2 Roast the fennel and mustard seeds in hot sunflower oil. Chop the garlic, cut the chilli in halves, remove the seeds and chop finely. Add garlic, chilli and potatoes to the seeds and cook briefly on low temperature. Add the spices, cook briefly, then add the water.

3 Roll out the dough to a thickness of 2-3 mm and cut into 8 × 8 cm squares with the pastry cutter. Brush the dough with the lightly whisked egg and spoon the filling of one half of each square. Fold the squares in half to form triangles. Press the edges down well with a fork and trim with the pastry cutter. Gather the trimmed edges, knead into a ball and roll out to make another samosa.

4 Fry the samosas in hot oil for 4-6 minutes until golden brown, or brush with egg yolk and bake in the oven at 190°C for about 15 minutes.

Tip: samosa or chapati dough is available in all good Indian or Asian export shops. You can also use puff pastry, at a pinch. If you wish to make your own dough, you can find the recipe in our book Hiltl: Virtuoso Vegetarian. If you like your samosas really hot, include the chilli seeds.

Makes approximately 45 samosas	600 g	potatoes	4 tsp garam masala
Preparation time	5 tbsp	sunflower oil	2 tsp turmeric
30 minutes	2 tsp	fennel seeds	fine sea salt
	6 tsp	black mustard seeds	200 ml water
	2	garlic cloves	1 kg samosa or chapati dough (see tip)
	1-2	green chillies	3 egg yolks, lightly whisked
	20	whole curry leaves	peanut oil for frying
	2 tsp	Jaffna curry	

Sit back and savour
the late summer evenings

relaxing

berry crumble

1 Roughly chop the biscuits and the walnuts in the food processor. Add sugar and oil, mix well and spread onto the base of a 15 × 20 cm gratin dish.
2 Wash and clean the berries, mix carefully with the jam and spread on top of the crumble mixture.
3 Mix the remaining ingredients in a stainless steel bowl into a compact mass, and spread on top of the berries.

4 Bake in the preheated oven at 180°C for 25-30 minutes until golden brown.

Tip: serve with a scoop of vanilla ice cream and garnish with fresh berries.

Preparation time	100 g	wholegrain biscuits	400 g	fresh berries (red currant, blueberries,
15 minutes	30 g	walnuts		raspberries and blackberries)
Baking time	1 tbsp	fine raw cane sugar	100 g	cherry or red berry jam
30 minutes	5 tbsp	rapeseed oil	150 g	Alpen muesli, no sugar added
			4 tbsp	raw cane sugar
			1-2 tbsp	rapeseed oil

73

auti

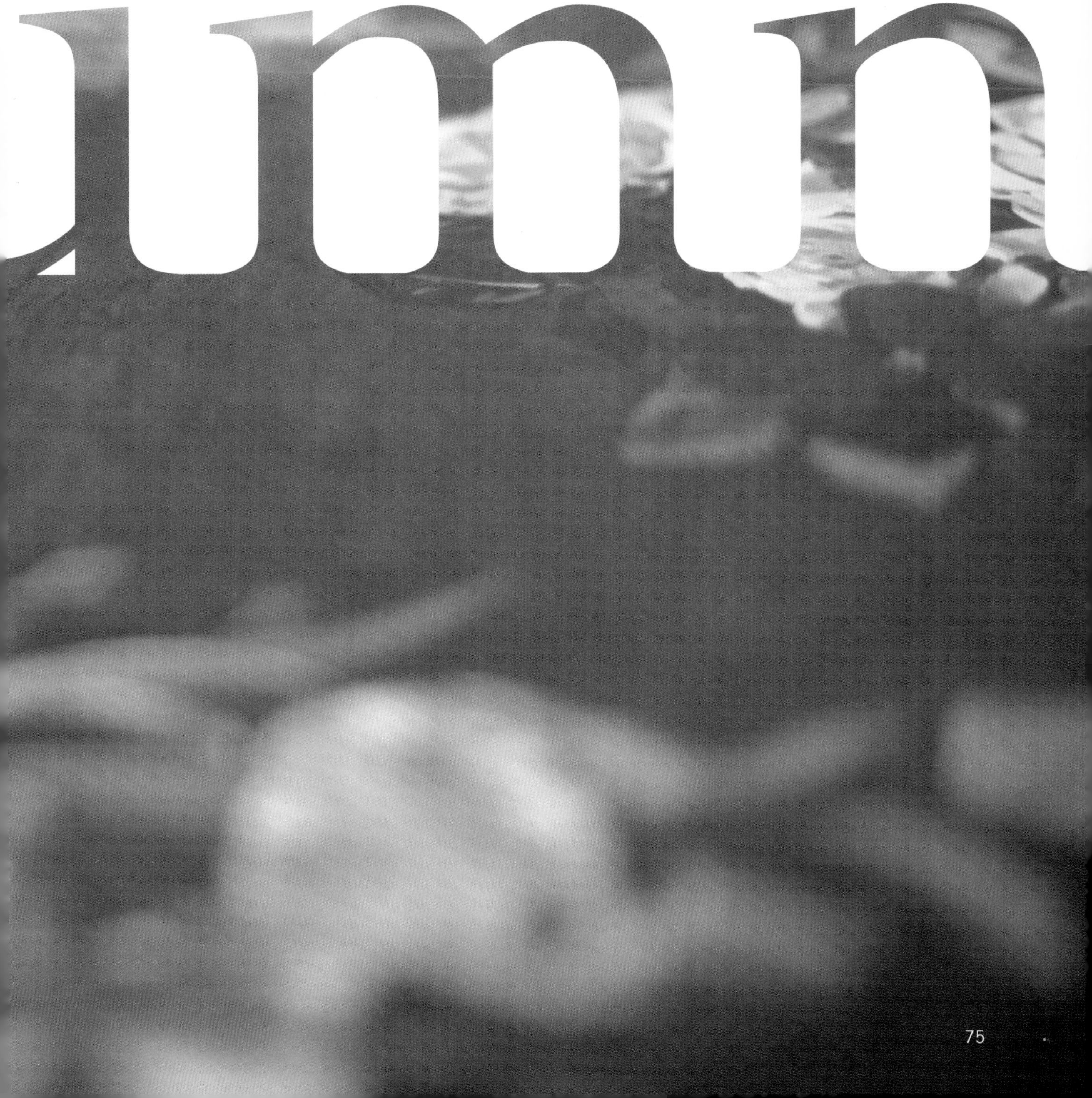

autumn light

When the days are getting shorter again, the leaves are falling and hats, gloves
and scarves come out of summer storage, we can't help but feel a little melancholic.
Suddenly our nose starts running once more. Smoke is coming out of the chimneys,
the parasols disappear from the verandas and it is no longer lovely outside.
Nature is turning from green to reddish-orange to brown and finally to a barren
black and for a little while, the balcony flowers are the only remaining dots of bright
colour outside. Autumn's colours are muted and we turn to the warm twilight indoors.
As our appetite comes back in force, we crave comfort food. Hot chestnuts,
pumpkins, beetroots, apples and potatoes come into their own.

A delicious and healthy drink cram-packed
with Vitamin B, potassium and iron

beetroot and passion fruit juice

1 Peel the bananas. Squeeze the lemon (you need
about 50 ml of juice).
2 Puree the bananas with the lemon juice and water
in the food processor.
3 Wash and peel the carrots and the beetroots and put
them in the juice extractor. Mix with the banana juice.

4 Cut the passion fruit in halves and scrape
the seeds and pulp into a bowl. Pass through a
fine sieve and mix with the juice.

Tip: sweeten to taste, with maple syrup.

Preparation time	2	bananas, peeled
10 minutes	1	lemon
	500 ml	water
	480 g	carrots
	150 g	beetroot
	12	passion fruit

Preparation time	300 g	potatoes	40 g	white quinoa
30 minutes	180 g	parsnips	500 ml	vegetable stock
	150 g	leek	300 ml	soy almond milk
	3 tbsp	rapeseed oil		freshly ground white pepper

leek and quinoa soup

1 Wash and peel potatoes and parsnips and chop into
1.5 cm dice. Wash the leek and chop into 1.5 cm squares.
2 Heat the oil in a cooking pot and briefly fry the quinoa
and the vegetables. Add the vegetable stock and the
soy milk and cook for 5 minutes. Turn down the heat and
let simmer for another 15-20 minutes. Season to taste,
with white pepper.

Preparation time	100 g	dried string beans	1	garlic clove
40 minutes		sea salt	80 g	walnuts
	½	onion	4 tbsp	balsamic vinegar
	8 tbsp	rapeseed oil		fresh coriander leaves
	60 ml	vegetable stock		

dried green bean salad

1 Put the beans in cold water with sea salt and bring to the boil. Simmer for 25 minutes until tender, but firm. Rinse immediately under cold running water, drain well and put into a bowl.

2 Finely chop the onion and sweat in hot rapeseed oil for 2 minutes. Deglaze with the vegetable stock, leave to cool.

3 Press the garlic and add to the beans with the onions, chopped walnuts and balsamic vinegar. Mix well and leave to marinate for 10 minutes.

4 Serve sprinkled with freshly chopped coriander.

Tip: if you put the beans into cold water for 2 hours before cooking, they will look less wrinkly. 100 g dried beans = 400 g cooked beans.

apple and ginger salad, with tofu

1 Wash the apples and cut into wedges. Remove the core and chop the wedges into 1.5 cm dice. Mix immediately with the lemon juice.

2 Remove the stems from the figs and roughly chop them. Add to the apples.

3 Chop the tofu into 1.5 cm dice and briefly fry in hot rapeseed oil, until golden brown. Leave to cool.

4 Mix the dressing ingredients, pour over the salad and mix well. Season to taste with fine sea salt and refrigerate.

5 Right before serving, mix well once more and garnish with fresh mint leaves.

Tip: the lemons will yield more juice if you wash them under warm running water and roll them back and forth on the work surface a few times, while pressing down gently.

We like to use Jonagold apples for their aromatic, sweet tartness but the choice of apples is a matter of personal taste.

Preparation time	500 g	apples (Jonagold)		Dressing	
20 minutes	1	lemon, juice (50 ml)		3	lemons, juice (150 ml)
	120 g	dried figs		20 g	freshly ground ginger
	250 g	tofu		4 tbsp	cane sugar
	8 tbsp	rapeseed oil		4 tbsp	sweet chilli sauce
					fine sea salt
				1 bunch	parsley, finely chopped

Our variation of the oriental
classic – a wonderful dip

hummus with red peppers and walnuts

1 Put the chickpeas into a sieve and rinse thoroughly under running water, then soak overnight in a bowl of water.
2 Drain the chickpeas and bring to the boil in fresh water, together with the spiced onion. Skim off the foam, then cook for 40 minutes until soft. Remove the onion. Drain, rinse in cold water, and drain again.
3 Wash the pepper, remove the seeds and cut into 4 pieces. Lay them skin side up on a baking tray and put under the hot grill until the skin begins to darken and detach. Cover with a kitchen towel and leave to cool, then remove the skin.

4 Puree the chickpeas and the pepper with the rapeseed oil, in the food processor.
5 Mix the chickpea paste with the remaining ingredients. If it is too thick, add a little water. Refrigerate until serving.
6 Serve garnished, with freshly chopped parsley.

Tip: serve the hummus with fresh Naan bread, pita bread or toasted baguette slices.

Preparation time	200 g	chickpeas, dried	1 tbsp	chilli oil
25 minutes	2 l	water for cooking	1 tsp	fine sea salt
Cooking time	1	onion, spiced with cloves and bay leaf	2	garlic cloves, pressed
40 minutes	3	red peppers	½ tsp	garam masala
	7 tbsp	rapeseed oil	½ tsp	cumin
	130 g	walnuts, ground	½ tsp	mild paprika powder
	3 tbsp	lemon juice	1 bunch	parsley

red rice salad

1 Bring the salted water to the boil, add the rice and cook for 30 minutes. Drain in a sieve and chill under running cold water. Rinse well.
2 Chop peppers and courgettes into 1 cm dice.
3 Wash the parsley, shake well and chop finely.
4 Put the remaining ingredients into a bowl and mix well, add the rice.
5 Add vegetables and parsley, mix well and refrigerate.

Tip: rice grown in the French Camargue region, gets its red colour from the high clay content of the soil. Camargue rice is untreated and unmilled 'brown' rice. It has a mild nutty flavour and stays grainy when cooked. Alternatively, you can use Riso Venere (Italian black rice) for this recipe.

Preparation time	160 g	camargue rice	1 tsp	fine sea salt
30 minutes	1	red and 1 yellow pepper	1 tbsp	tomato paste
	1	courgette	½ tsp	hot curry powder
	1 bunch	of parsley	½ tsp	mild paprika powder
	2 tbsp	rapeseed oil	½ tsp	ground coriander
	3 tbsp	white balsamic vinegar	½ tsp	cumin powder
	1 tsp	chilli oil		

A quintessential autumn food, the chestnut's
prickly exterior belies its delicious centre

attention to detail

A particularly delicious pasta dish,
with a sensational sauce

cavatappi pasta with courgettes curry sauce

1 Wash the courgettes and julienne: slice them lengthwise, then cut into fine 10 cm strips.
2 Bring soy milk and coconut milk to the boil. Mix the cornflour with the water, add to the sauce and cook for a few minutes until it thickens.
3 Mix the ginger with the spices, add to the sauce and simmer for a further minute.
4 Meanwhile, cook the pasta al dente in plenty of salted water and drain well. Add the drained pasta and the courgette julienne to the sauce, bring to the boil and season with salt and pepper. Serve immediately.

Tip: you can use whole milk instead of soy milk. Cavatappi, also called cellentani, are short hollow pasta spirals (similar to macaroni). They usually have small grooves outside.

Preparation time	Sauce		50 g	ginger, freshly grated	250 g	cavatappi or similar pasta
20 minutes	200 g	courgettes	1 tsp	mustard seed		freshly ground fine sea salt
	250 ml	soy milk	½ tsp	cumin powder		and black pepper
	250 ml	coconut milk	½ tsp	ground coriander		
	2 tbsp	cornflour	½ tsp	garam masala		
	4 tbsp	water	1 tsp	turmeric		

goa curry

1 Remove the stem end and peel the pineapple.
Cut the flesh into 1.5 cm dice.
2 Peel the onion and the pearl onions. Cut the chilli
pepper in half lengthwise and remove the seeds,
finely chop chilli and onion.
3 Chop the tofu into 1.5 cm dice.
4 Heat 8 tablespoons of rapeseed oil in a frying pan
and lightly fry the onion, chilli, pineapple and pearl
onions for 5 minutes.

5 Heat 4 tablespoons of rapeseed oil in another pan
and quickly fry the tofu until lightly brown. Add to the
pineapple mixture.
6 Mix the sauce ingredients in a wide pan, bring to
the boil and lightly reduce the liquid for about 2 minutes.
Add the pineapple-tofu mixture and cook for another
5 minutes.
7 Serve with basmati rice (recipe on p136) and sprinkle
with toasted coconut flakes.

Preparation time	¼	pineapple (250 g)		Sauce		½ tsp	curry powder
40 minutes	1	onion	120 ml	vegetable stock		½ tsp	mild paprika powder
	100 g	pearl onions	280 ml	coconut milk		½ tsp	ground coriander
	80 g	green chilli	2 tbsp	green curry paste		½ tsp	cumin powder
	200 g	tofu	1 tbsp	freshly ground ginger		½ tsp	cinnamon
	120 ml	rapeseed oil	1 tsp	fine sea salt		30 g	toasted coconut flakes
			1 tbsp	tomato paste			

A Creole recipe, created by
our London head chef

vegetable jambalaya

1 Cook the rice in saltwater, for about 20 minutes.
2 Wash the vegetables and chop into 1.5 cm dice.
3 Finely chop the onion and cut the garlic into fine slices. Stir-fry the garlic, onion and vegetables in the rapeseed oil for 7-9 minutes. Then add the spices and cook until the vegetables are tender but firm.

4 Drain the rice, add to the vegetables and mix well.
5 Wash the tomatoes, chop into 1.5 cm dice and scatter over the dish, just before serving.

Tip: you can also use different vegetables like snow peas, okra, green beans or maize.

Preparation time	200 g	long grain rice	1 pinch	of cayenne pepper
30 minutes	150 g	aubergines	2 tsp	fine sea salt
	150 g	butternut squash	1 tsp	fresh thyme
	150 g	red and green peppers	2	bay leaves
	150 g	courgettes	1-2 tsp	sambal oelek
	1	onion	200 g	tomatoes
	2	garlic cloves		
	8 tbsp	rapeseed oil		

yellow pea vadai

1 Soak the yellow peas in water over night, then drain, rinse briefly and leave to drain. Puree finely, in the food processor.
2 Finely chop the onion and garlic, cut the chilli in half, remove the seeds and chop finely. Chop the curry leaves.
3 Work all ingredients into a smooth dough. With your hands, shape walnut sized balls and place on a sheet of lightly oiled baking paper.

4 Heat the oil to 160°C and deep fry the vadai in several batches for about 4-6 minutes. Leave to drain on paper towels.

Tip: serve with a dollop of chutney. You will find another delicious vadai recipe in Hiltl: Virtuoso Vegetarian.

Preparation time	200 g	yellow peas	1 tsp	freshly ground white pepper
20 minutes	1	onion	2 tbsp	hot curry powder
	2	garlic cloves	1 tbsp	fine sea salt
	2-3	green chilli		rapeseed oil for deep frying
	4-5	fresh curry leaves		

Enjoying a lazy evening on the sofa,
is truly one of life's simple pleasures

Preparation time	6	eggs	140 g	almonds, ground	2 tbsp	cornflour
for a 30 cm bread loaf pan	150 g	butter, at room temperature	220 g	poppy seeds		butter and
30 minutes	150 g	raw cane sugar	1 tsp	baking powder		almond flakes,
Baking time	1 tsp	salt	80 g	raw cane sugar		for baking
60 minutes						

poppy seed cake

1 Separate the eggs.
2 Whisk the egg yolks with the butter and salt, until creamy.
3 Mix the almonds, poppy seeds and baking powder.
4 Whisk the egg white with the second portion of sugar until stiff, then fold in the cornflour. Fold the stiff egg white and the almond poppy seed mix carefully into the butter mix.

5 Brush a baking pan with butter and sprinkle with almond flakes or line with baking paper. Spoon the batter into the pan and cook in a preheated oven at 160-180 °C, for approximately 60 minutes.

Tip: for a more intense flavour, roast the poppy seeds and the ground almonds in the oven at 170 °C for about 8 minutes. The cake will keep fresh in the refrigerator for around one week.

Preparation time	125 ml water	5 tsp cornflour
15 minutes	250 ml coconut milk	2.5 tbsp cold water
	125 g cocoa powder, sweetened	150 ml whipping cream
	4 tbsp raw cane sugar	

coconut chocolate pudding

1 Bring the water, coconut milk, cocoa powder and sugar
to the boil. Mix the cornflour with the cold water, add
to the pot and cook until the pudding has thickened.
Pour into a bowl, cover with cling film and refrigerate.
2 When cold, whip the pudding with the hand blender
until creamy.
3 Whip the cream and carefully fold into the pudding.

nter

winter wonderland

The winter takes no prisoners. Below zero temperatures and inclement weather,
have brought life outside to a grinding halt. Our home seems especially inviting now.
We light a fire and pass the long winter hours curled up on the sofa reading a good
book or watching all the films we did not get a chance to see during the summer.
A glass of hot punch brings a glow to cold cheeks and restores movement to frostbitten
fingers. But just because we are hunkering down at home now, does not mean that
we are living the life of a recluse. Winter is the time for dinner parties and putting the
world to rights, over a glass (or two) of wine. Nothing beats gathering around a lovely
laid table for a home-cooked meal, when there is a howling winter gale outside.

A great immune booster – warming in
the winter and refreshing in the summer!

ginger lemon punch

1 Peel the ginger and chop roughly. Squeeze the lemons (you need 120 ml of juice).

2 Mix all ingredients in the food processor on full speed, for about 5 minutes. Leave to settle for a few minutes, then pass through a fine sieve and refrigerate.

3 Serve hot: pour into a cup and top up with hot water. Garnish with a slice of lemon.

4 Serve cold: pour into a glass with ice cubes, top up with sparkling mineral water and garnish with a slice of lemon.

Serves 6	ginger syrup	Served hot, per serving	Served cold, per serving
Preparation time	80 g ginger, peeled and chopped	5 tbsp ginger lemon syrup	5 tbsp ginger lemon syrup
15 minutes	3 lemons	1 cup of hot water	ice cubes
	6 tbsp sugar	1 slice of lemon	sparkling mineral water
	8 tbsp elderberry syrup		1 slice of lemon
	4 tbsp water		

Preparation time	600 g white cabbage	Dressing
20 minutes	350 g carrots	150 g rice mayonnaise (see tip)
		120 g plain yoghurt
		5 tbsp white balsamic vinegar
		4 tbsp peach and passion fruit syrup

coleslaw

1 Wash the cabbage and carrots. Peel the carrots. Grate both into fine strips using a vegetable slicer.
2 Mix the dressing ingredients in a large bowl, add the vegetables and mix well. Refrigerate for 1 hour.

Tip: rice mayonnaise is prepared with rice instead of eggs and therefore suitable for vegans. You can buy it in health food shops.
Instead of the peach and passion fruit syrup, you can use any other syrup, such as orange, elderflower or apricot syrup. All are available in health food shops.

Preparation time	300 g	parsnips	600 ml	vegetable stock
20 minutes	200 g	potatoes	100 ml	soy milk
	3	shallots	½	lemon, juice
	1	garlic clove		freshly ground sea salt and white pepper
	2 tbsp	extra virgin olive oil	½ bunch	of majoram

parsnip soup

1 Wash the parsnips and potatoes, peel and chop into 2 cm dice. Peel and finely chop shallots and garlic.
2 Heat the olive oil in a cooking pan and sweat the vegetables for a few minutes. Add the vegetable stock and soy milk and simmer for 10 minutes, until the vegetables are tender.
3 Puree the soup in the food processor or with a hand blender and pass through a fine sieve.
4 Add the lemon juice and bring the soup to the boil again. Season to taste with salt and pepper and serve sprinkled with fresh marjoram leaves.

Tip: parsnips look rather like carrots but they are yellowish-white in colour. Their slightly bittersweet taste is reminiscent of carrots, celeriac or parsley root.

111

thai coconut soup

1 Peel and finely chop the onions and garlic. Squash the lemongrass on a chopping board. Finely chop the lemongrass and kaffir lime leaves. Cut the chilli in half lengthwise, remove the seeds and cut into thin strips. Peel galangal and ginger and cut into thin slices. Wash and squeeze the limes.
2 Heat the rapeseed oil and sweat the onion, garlic, lemongrass, kaffir lime leaves, chilli and galangal until the onion is transparent.
3 Add vegetable stock, coconut milk, lime juice, ginger and cane sugar and cook for 10 minutes, at a low temperature.

4 Puree the soup in the food processor, or with a hand blender, and pass through a sieve.
5 Bring the soup to the boil again. Mix the cornflour with the cold water, add to the soup and cook for approximately 1 minute until it thickens. Serve hot, sprinkled with fresh coriander leaves.

Tip: serve the soup with some baby corn or use fresh Thai basil, instead of coriander.
Galangal, also called blue ginger, is a popular ingredient in Thai cuisine and in natural medicine. The rhizome has a slightly bitter, aromatic taste and stimulates digestion.

Preparation time		
25 minutes	1	small onion
	2	garlic cloves
	2 stalks	lemongrass
	4-5	kaffir lime leaves
	3	red chillies
	50 g	galangal
	50 g	ginger
	2	limes
	3 tbsp	rapeseed oil

500 ml	vegetable stock
500 ml	coconut milk
1 tsp	raw can sugar
1 tbsp	cornflour
1 tbsp	cold water
½ bunch	coriander (cilantro)

A light salad, delicious and very attractive

black quinoa with cherry tomatoes

1 Bring the salted water to the boil, add the quinoa and cook for 20 minutes. Drain well.
2 Wash the vegetables. Remove the cucumber and chilli seeds, then cut into 1 cm dice. Cut each cherry tomato into 4 pieces.
3 Mix the sauce ingredients and add the quinoa.
4 Add tomatoes, cucumber and chilli and mix well.

Tip: prepare the quinoa the night before and put into the refrigerator to drain and cool down.

Preparation time	100 g black quinoa	Sauce
30 minutes	½ red and ½ yellow pepper	2.5 tbsp extra virgin olive oil
	½ cucumber	3 tbsp sweet chilli sauce
	100 g cherry tomatoes	2.5 tbsp white balsamic vinegar
		1 tsp fine sea salt

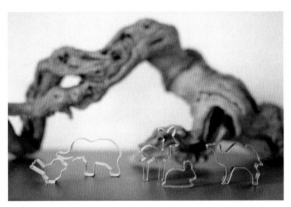

Nourish your mind,
body and soul at home

117

One of the finest lentil varieties and like
all lentils, an excellent source of protein

beluga lentil salad

1 Cook the lentils in salted water, for about 18 minutes.
2 Wash and peel the carrots and chop into 1 cm dice.
Add to the lentils and cook for another 2 minutes, then
drain immediately. Rinse under running cold water
and drain well.
3 Wash the courgettes, chop into 1 cm dice and add
to the lentils.
4 Finely chop the sundried tomatoes. Mix all remaining
dressing ingredients and add the chopped tomatoes.
5 Mix the lentils with the dressing and season to taste,
with salt and pepper.

Tip: these small, black lentils glisten when they
cook, which makes them look like Beluga caviar.
Since they do not disintegrate when cooked, they work
equally well in appetisers, side dishes or as garnish.
Tikka curry paste is a popular ingredient in Northern
Indian cuisine and mainly used for sauces and
marinades. Add some olive oil if desired.

Preparation time	200 g	beluga lentils		Dressing	
30 minutes	2	carrots		60 g	sundried tomatoes in oil
	2	courgettes		20 g	ginger, freshly ground
				6 tbsp	extra virgin olive oil
				6 tbsp	white balsamic vinegar
				2 tbsp	Tikka curry paste (see tip)
				1 tbsp	chilli oil
					freshly ground fine sea salt
					and white pepper

warm dal with spinach

1 Cook the lentils for about 8 minutes, in salted water. Drain.

2 Peel and finely chop the onion and garlic. Peel the ginger and grate finely. Heat a frying pan, then add the oil and sweat the onion until transparent. Add the garlic, ginger and spices and fry for 1 minute, until the mixture develops its fragrance.

3 Wash and pluck the spinach, add to the pan and cook for 2-3 minutes.

4 Add coconut milk and water, and stir well.

5 Add the drained lentils, mix in well and cook for a further 5 minutes.

6 Season to taste with sea salt, freshly ground black pepper and lemon juice.

Preparation time	250 g	red lentils	1 tsp	turmeric
30 minutes	1	onion	500 g	fresh spinach
	1	garlic clove	400 ml	coconut milk
	20 g	ginger	200 ml	water
	4 tbsp	rapeseed oil		freshly ground sea salt
	1 tsp	mustard seeds		and black pepper
	½ tsp	cumin	½	lemon, juice
	½ tsp	ground coriander		
	½ tsp	garam masala		

A perfect pasta dish for the winter season!

linguini with pumpkin and swiss chard

1 Wash the lemons, peel the zest and cut into very fine strips. Squeeze the lemons (you need 50 ml juice).
2 Peel the pumpkin and cut lengthwise into 3 mm thin slices, then cut the slices into fine 10 cm strips.
3 Wash the chard and cut the stem and leaves into fine strips. Put into a mixture of milk and water, until needed.
4 Bring the cream, milk, vegetable stock and chilli oil to the boil. Mix the cornflour with the cold water, add to the liquid and cook for about 1 minute, until it thickens.

5 Break the linguini in two and cook in plenty of saltwater until al dente. Drain well.
6 Put the drained pasta, pumpkin, drained chard and lemon zest into the sauce, mix well and bring to the boil again. Season with salt, pepper and lemon juice and serve immediately.

Tip: linguini ("little tongues") are like flattened spaghetti. You can also use taglierini.

Preparation time	1-2	lemons	1 tbsp	cornflour
20 minutes	¼	butternut squash	1 tbsp	water
	200 g	Swiss chard, milk and water	300 g	linguini (or another type
	200 ml	double cream		of ribbon pasta)
	300 ml	milk		freshly ground sea salt
	100 ml	vegetable stock		and white pepper
	1 tsp	chilli oil .		

This recipe takes a little time to prepare,
but the result is well worth any effort involved!

spelt risotto
with mushrooms

1 Wash and drain the spelt.
2 Finely chop the onion and sweat in the rapeseed oil, until transparent. Add the spelt, fry for a few minutes, then add the vegetable stock. Cook at low temperature for about 50 minutes stirring occasionally, until the spelt has absorbed all the liquid.
3 Clean the mushrooms, cut into slices and cook in the rapeseed oil. Add the chilli oil and deglaze with the vegetable stock. Add the cream and allow the liquid to reduce a little.

4 Add the mushrooms to the spelt, bring to the boil again, stirring all the while, then cook for another 3 minutes. Add the grated cheese and the freshly chopped parsley and serve immediately.

Tip: you can prepare the spelt the night before. Instead of cream, use soy cream. HOLL (High Oleic Low Linolenic) rapeseed oil has a higher percentage of oleic acid and a lower percentage of linolenic acid, than ordinary rapeseed oil. It is very heat resistant and therefore ideal for frying. Cold pressed oil has a more intensive colour and taste, but does not keep as well as hot-pressed oil.

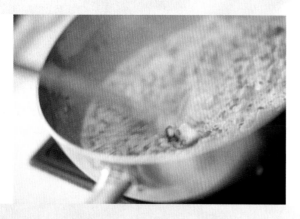

Preparation time	250 g spelt	250 g mushrooms	50 g cheese (such as Gruyere
60 minutes	1 onion	4 tbsp rapeseed oil	or Emmental), grated
	4 tbsp rapeseed oil	½ tsp chilli oil	1 bunch parsley, chopped
	1.2 l vegetable stock	125 ml vegetable stock	
		200 ml whipping cream	

spinach and feta lasagne

1 Grate the feta cheese roughly on a cheese grater. Cut the tomatoes into 0.5 cm slices.

2 Wash the spinach and remove the stalks. Peel the onion and chop finely.

3 Heat a frying pan, add the oil and sweat the onion until transparent. Add the spinach and cook for 2-3 minutes. Season with salt and pepper.

4 Bring soy milk, vegetable stock and chilli oil to the boil. Mix the cornflour with the cold water, add to the liquid and cook for about 1 minute until it thickens.

5 Assemble the lasagne in a 15 × 22 cm gratin dish: 200 g sauce; a layer of pasta; half of the spinach and half of the feta cheese; a layer of pasta; 300 g sauce, the remaining spinach and the tomato slices; a layer of pasta, followed by the remaining sauce and feta cheese.

6 Prick the lasagne a few times with a sharp knife (this prevents the lasagne from inflating while cooking). Bake in a preheated oven at 180°C for 25-30 minutes.

Preparation time	160 g feta cheese	250 ml vegetable stock
60 minutes	200 g tomatoes	½ tsp chilli oil
	500 g fresh spinach	4-5 tsp cornflour
	1 onion	8 tbsp cold water
	4 tbsp rapeseed oil	200 g fresh green lasagne sheets
	550 ml soy milk	

Candles help create a cosy atmosphere in your home, through their warmth and accent lighting

luminous

banana crème with vanilla and turmeric

1 Bring the milk, sugar and scraped-out vanilla pulp to the boil. Mix the cornflour with the cold water, add to the liquid and cook for about 1 minute until it thickens.
2 Pour the pudding into a bowl, cover with cling-film and refrigerate for 1 hour.
3 Mash the bananas thoroughly by hand, or with a hand blender and mix well with the pudding.

4 Whip the cream until stiff and carefully fold into the pudding. Refrigerate until serving.

Tip: you can add the vanilla pods to the milk and remove after cooking. Alternatively, put them in a glass container with sugar and close the lid tightly. The sugar will take on a subtle vanilla taste.

Preparation time	200 ml	milk
20 minutes	50 g	raw cane sugar
	1 tsp	turmeric
	2	bourbon vanilla pods
	2 tbsp	cornflour
	2 tbsp	water
	300 g	peeled bananas
	120 ml	whipping cream

A sweet delight for grown ups and children alike!

chocolate and coconut macaroons

1 Preheat the oven to 150°C.
2 Mix the caster sugar, with the vanilla sugar. Finely grate the chocolate.
3 Separate the eggs. Whip the egg whites until very stiff while drizzling the sugar into the mixture.
4 Carefully fold the chocolate and coconut flakes into the whipped egg white.
5 Spoon the batter into a pastry bag with a star tip and pipe small macaroons onto a baking tray, lined with baking paper. Alternatively, make small heaps of batter with two wet teaspoons. Bake for 15-20 minutes. Remove the tray from the oven and leave to cool completely before removing the macaroons from the paper.

Tip: for a more intense chocolate flavour, melt the chocolate in a bain-marie (water bath). Leave to cool at room temperature, before folding into the beaten egg whites.

Makes 30-40 macaroons

Preparation time
15 minutes

2 eggs

160 g caster sugar

5 g vanilla sugar

100 g dark chocolate
(45 per cent cocoa content, minimum)

160 g coconut flakes

basic recipes

Chilli and orange dressing

1 Wash and squeeze the oranges (you need 300 ml juice).
2 Mix the rice mayonnaise, orange juice and the remaining ingredients in the food processor for about 1 minute.
3 Refrigerate. The dressing will keep fresh for about 5 days.

Makes 1 litre
Preparation time
10 minutes

4-5	oranges
350 g	rice mayonnaise (available in health food shops, see tip on p110)
70 ml	white balsamic vinegar
160 ml	rapeseed oil
100 ml	sambal oelek
40 g	raw cane sugar

Tomato pesto

1 Peel the garlic. Drain the sundried tomatoes.
2 Puree all ingredients in the food processor.
3 Fill into screw-top glasses and keep in the refrigerator.

Makes 500 g
Preparation time
10 minutes

4	garlic cloves
150 g	sundried tomatoes, in oil
120 ml	extra virgin olive oil
8 tbsp	sunflower oil
140 g	tomato paste
½ tsp	ground galangal

Basmati rice with herbs

1 Rinse the rice under cold running water and drain well.
2 Stir the spices into the water, add the rice and bring to the boil.
3 Cover the pot and simmer for 12-15 minutes. Do not stir.
4 Remove the pot from the stove and leave for 5 minutes. Remove cinnamon stick and cloves, and break up the rice with a fork.

Preparation time
20 minutes

250 g	basmati rice
420 ml	water
2 tbsp	rapeseed oil
	fine sea salt
½	cinnamon stick
2	cloves
½ tsp	turmeric
½ tsp	ground coriander

Home made vegetable stock

1 Wash the vegetables and chop roughly.
2 Heat the oil in a large cooking pot. Quickly fry the carrots, onions, fennel and celeriac until golden brown. Add the cabbage, leek, spices and bay leaf and fry until the aroma unfolds. Add the herbs and deglaze with the water. Bring to the boil and simmer for 45 minutes, then add the sea salt and stir until it has completely dissolved.
3 Pour the stock through a sieve and fill immediately into sterilised glass containers. The stock will keep in the refrigerator for about 2 weeks.

Tip: use the stock as a base for soups and sauces and for deglazing. This recipe was first published in 'Hiltl. Veggie International. A World of Difference.' Making a few incisions into the bay leaves with a pair of kitchen scissors, will allow more of the aroma to infuse into the stock. Cooking the onion with the peel, makes the stock nicely golden brown.

Makes 3.5 litres
Preparation time
60 minutes

1	carrot
2	onions, unpeeled
½	fennel bulb
½	small celeriac root
1	small leek
¼	small savoy cabbage
2 tbsp	rapeseed oil
1 tbsp	black peppercorns
1 tsp	fennel seeds
1 tsp	brown mustard seeds
1 tsp	caraway seeds
2	bay leaves
4 sprigs	parsley
1 sprig	rosemary
1 sprig	tarragon
4 l	water
2 tbsp	fine sea salt

Spelt dough

1 Thoroughly mix the flour, with the olive oil. Add water and a little sea salt and work into smooth dough. Put into the refrigerator for 1 hour.
2 Roll out the dough onto a sheet of baking paper, the size of the baking tray. Place the dough on the paper, onto the tray, and lightly press down the edges with your fingers.

Tip: this makes an excellent quiche base.

Preparation time
10 minutes

150 g	spelt flour (type 1050)
75 ml	olive oil
75 ml	water, room temperature
	fine sea salt

By Bettina Weber

tibits – when vegetarian food makes you happy

Three brothers

Once, there were three bright young brothers from the Rhine valley, near St. Gallen, who did not eat meat. Not even as teenagers. Given that this was the 1970s when meat was considered a necessary part of a meal, this was simply unheard of. However Reto, Daniel and Christian Frei refused to eat meat for ethical reasons. This has never changed. And although social awareness has evolved since then, one thing has stayed the same: men are in charge of the barbecue. Men like steaks. But the Frei brothers beg to differ. Their mother, an Italian, taught the trio to cook and to love food. And you can be passionate about good food, even if you are a vegetarian. The brothers' keen interest in vegetarian cuisine has made them the successful entrepreneurs that they are today. They are successful because they know how to enjoy.

Idea versus preconceived notion

While reading business economics at the ETH Zurich (Swiss Federal Institute of Technology Zurich), a fellow student talked Reto Frei into attending a lecture he had planned to skip. The lecture was promoting a business plan competition run by the university, in cooperation with the managing consultancy McKinsey. Reto Frei listened intently to the lecture and decided that he liked the idea of establishing a company. He consulted his brothers and together, they quickly came up with the concept for a vegetarian fast food restaurant. This idea was not entirely altruistic because back then, conventional restaurants only offered vegetarians (like the Frei brothers) uninspiring side dishes or tomato mozzarella sandwiches. Vegetarians were viewed as nit pickers and heath freaks, in short, they were seen as killjoys. But for the Frei brothers, nothing could be further from the truth: they simply loved eating well, far too much for that.

Enjoying good food

The idea for their vegetarian restaurant, therefore, was not focused on the absence of meat but on the love of good food. Precisely because they were so aware of all the preconceived notions about vegetarians, the brothers tried to avoid all attempts to moralise. It was not their aim to convert their customers to vegetarianism, but to provide a delicious alternative to meat. They were sure that they were not the only ones who loved a healthy, meat free meal for lunch, dinner or simply as a snack – something that was not just sustenance but sheer delight.

They began 'Project V' with street surveys, starting with four apparently harmless questions until springing the crucial one on the unsuspecting audience: "Would you eat in a vegetarian restaurant?" The answers they received were surprisingly positive, particularly among women. Men still tended to turn up their nose, considering vegetarians "a tad strange". Preconceptions, after all, are persistent.

But 'Project V' managed to convince the jury, among them such august members as Fritz Fahrni, then CEO of the Sulzer Corporation, and Franz Humer (CEO of the pharmaceutical group, Roche). Out of 200 competitors, they made the list of 11 finalists and received two awards.

The leek photograph

And then Rolf Hiltl entered the picture. In 1898, Hiltl's great-grandparents had brought vegetarian cuisine to Zurich, establishing what according to the Guinness Book of World Records, was the very first vegetarian restaurant in in the world. 'Rolf Hiltl read about the project in the newspaper and looked at the photograph of Reto and Christian Frei holding an enormous leek and beaming for the cameras. He was immediately captivated by the brothers and their idea, having had the same thought years ago but lacked the time to establish a fast food style restaurant, next to Hiltl. But this project, Hiltl thought, was promising so he sent the Frei brothers an email, proposing a meeting.

(From left) Christian, Daniel (standing) and Reto Frei and Rolf Hiltl

139

A stroke of good fortune

The email was well received because the brothers were, in fact, searching for a professional restaurateur. Particularly a professional who could offer exactly the kind of expertise they were after: high quality vegetarian cuisine. The Frei brothers and Rolf Hiltl hit it off immediately, coming from the same place in terms of goals and attitude. Despite or perhaps precisely, because they are all very different from each other – Reto is the boffin, Daniel the administrator, Christian the creative spirit and Rolf Hiltl the consummate gastronomer – they have become the dream team, complementing each other perfectly. From the very start, it was clear that the setting should be relaxed, not formal. The focus was to be a sumptuous buffet in the centre, accessible from all sides (to avoid queuing), with dishes to be sold by weight. Although basically a fast food restaurant, the setting needed to be stylish and calm. And another thing was clear from the beginning: the restaurant would be open all day, not just for lunch. The setting should be charming and comfortable enough for clients to want to spend time in it. So the team contacted Tricia Guild, renowned designer and founder of the famous interior decorating company, Designers Guild. And very soon, things started to happen. 'Project V' became 'tibits', a pun on 'titbits', which is exactly what this restaurant has to offer: a selection of small, delicious titbits making for a light and nutritious meal.

Always tongue in cheek

Before the project started in earnest, the Frei brothers closely cooperated with Rolf Hiltl in order to familiarise themselves with the restaurant business. During that time, Reto graduated from university, Daniel worked in the strategic development department of a large company and Christian was running his own private school.

But when the restaurant opened, they all threw themselves into the task of running a full time restaurant, doing all the jobs that were required in this type of business. No chore was beneath them and their enthusiasm was contagious. But in hindsight, they all agree that at times they were a little overcome by the enormity of the task. They simply had not expected the level of success they had. From the word go, customers took to tibits. So what was the big secret, the key to their success? It was the brothers' passion for good, fresh, healthy and fun food and the desire to make people welcome. And last but not least, their particular brand of advertising: never proselytizing and always a little tongue in cheek.

Fast forward to today and the current clientele does not consist solely of women. More and more men are now frequenting tibits. After all, where better to meet women, than in a beautiful setting with a large choice of high quality vegetarian gourmet food?! We rest our case.

tibits in Zurich since December 2000

Photo: tibits

Ahead of their time

Of course, the Frei brothers and Rolf Hiltl were far ahead of their time. Sustainability, now a buzzword, had been a way of life for them when no one even knew what it meant. However you will not find the company's green credentials, on the tibits website. Customers do not need to read about the owners' good intentions, when these are already evident in each and every tibits restaurant. When you do ask them for their credo, they simply say: "Enjoy life. Trust. Look ahead. Take your time".

When controversy arose in Zurich as to whether mothers should be allowed to breastfeed their babies in restaurants, their response was: "We were all babies once." As such, you'll find a mother and child corner in all tibits restaurants, as well as an area for breastfeeding: everyone is welcome. And you only need to have a look at the clientele to know that this is true: heavily tattooed bikers in leather gear mingle with the more customary patrons such as students, graphic designers, journalists, bank clerks, and pensioners alike.

More than a trend

Nowadays, there is a plethora of books on the vegetarian way of life. Vegetarianism has become much more mainstream, and a growing number of people understand that foregoing meat does not mean foregoing pleasure. On the contrary, it can be a very positive experience. You are not only good to yourself but to your environment. The Frei brothers and Rolf Hiltl have been benefitting from this trend and are very happy about the way things seem to be going as, from a business point of view, it proves that their project is not just a passing fancy. The passion for good food with fresh and healthy ingredients, is universal. And it is here to stay.

The expansion

Although trying to eat at tibits during rush hour can be a bit of a squeeze, expansion is not the answer for the entrepreneurs. Neither the Frei brothers nor Rolf Hiltl want to lose sight of their objectives, in the heady times of success. There are to date only five tibits restaurants in Switzerland; two in Zurich and one apiece in Winterthur, Basle and Berne. Yet when it comes to 'branching out', only the most daring venue will do: London, of all places, where the choice of good food is absolutely gigantic, where there is vicious competition between restaurant owners – this is where tibits wanted to test the waters. Not surprisingly, it took three years to find a suitable location and it took long hours of negotiations and setbacks before the Frei brothers were finally able to sign on the dotted line. But it happened. The London outpost is located in Heddon Street: a prime W1 venue just off Regent Street. But there was struggle ahead. Londoners did not prove to be as open to vegetarian food as anticipated, suffering from the misconception that veggie dining is dull and spartan.

Yet in the end, it only took a year for Londoners to embrace this green gourmet venture and today herbivores and the staunchest of carnivores alike can be seen sitting side by side in tibits' stunning environs, enjoying a mouthwatering meat free meze. A green gourmet is underway in the UK – keep checking the tibits website for the low-down on new locations!

tibits in London since October 2008

Photo: tibits

141

the recipes

Sweets, puddings and drinks

Basic recipes

142

10 years of tibits
advertisements:
a feast for the eyes

UNDERGROUND

Very Fresh Vegetarian Cuisine.

tibits

Vegetarian Fast Food. tibits

Vegetarian Fast Food. tibits

Veggie Conquers London. tibits

Very Fresh Vegetarian Food. tibits

Vegetarian Take Away.

Eat Yourself Fit. tibits

Fresh Instead Of Foul.

tibits

Vegetarian Paradise. tibits

Prima ballerinas eat at tibits.

Meat won't get through to our plates. tibits

Very Fresh Vegetarian Cuisine.

Very Fresh Vegetarian Cuis

Appropriate Keeping Of Tea. tibits

Enjoy our selection of tibits ads.

tibits

Veggie Wins tibits

Veggie Wins tibits

Veggie Conquers London. tibits

143

Photo: wirz.ch

Hiltl: since 1898

According to the Guinness Book of World Records, the Hiltl restaurant in Zurich is the oldest vegetarian restaurant in the world. It was established by Ambrosius Hiltl in 1898 and has been in the hands of the Hiltl family for four consecutive generations. In the centre of the restaurant, there is a large buffet with a daily choice of more than 100 home made specialities. Over 30 chefs prepare the dishes with fresh ingredients daily, in the large open-plan kitchen. They are sold according to weight and are also available to take away. There is also a traditional a la carte restaurant and a patisserie, lounge bar and 'Club Hiltl' in addition to a cookery school, a catering section and a shop. More information at www.hiltl.ch/en

Cookery books by Hiltl

To celebrate its 100 year-anniversary in 1998, Hiltl published 'Hiltl. Virtuoso Vegetarian', which has since become a classic.
For its 111th birthday, Hiltl launched 'Hiltl. Veggie International. A World of Difference'. Both books are available in the tibits and Hiltl restaurants, as well as in bookshops in the UK and in Switzerland and on the internet.

Cooperation with tibits

tibits is following in the footsteps of over a century old tradition of the Hiltl establishment. They share certain key features, such as the central buffet and the freshly prepared fruit juices. Both family enterprises are constantly developing new products and strategies, which are shared in partnership. The Frei brothers and Rolf Hiltl equally own one half of the shares of tibits Ltd. The company is run by the Frei family with Rolf and Marielle Hiltl on the board of managing directors.

Photo: hiltl